Life Skills Every 11 Year Old Should Know

Unlock Your Secret Superpowers and Succeed in All Areas of Life

Hayden Fox

1

© Copyright - All rights reserved.

The content contained within this book may not be reproduced, duplicated or transmitted without direct written permission from the author or the publisher.

Under no circumstances will any blame or legal responsibility be held against the publisher, or author, for any damages, reparation, or monetary loss due to the information contained within this book, either directly or indirectly.

Legal Notice:

This book is copyright protected. It is only for personal use. You cannot amend, distribute, sell, use, quote or paraphrase any part, or the content within this book, without the consent of the author or publisher.

Disclaimer Notice:

Please note the information contained within this document is for educational and entertainment purposes only. All effort has been executed to present accurate, up to date, reliable, complete information. No warranties of any kind are declared or implied. Readers acknowledge that the author is not engaged in the rendering of legal, financial, medical or professional advice. The content within this book has been derived from various sources. Please consult a licensed professional before attempting any techniques outlined in this book.

By reading this document, the reader agrees that under no circumstances is the author responsible for any losses, direct or indirect, that are incurred as a result of the use of the information contained within this document, including, but not limited to, errors, omissions, or inaccuracies.

Claim your free gifts!

(My way of saying thank you for your support)

Simply visit **haydenfoxmedia.com** to receive the following:

- 10 Powerful Dinner Conversations To Create Amazing Kids

- 10 Magical Affirmations To Help Kids Become Unstoppable in Life

(you can also scan this QR code)

This book belongs to

to

_____

Table of Contents

Introduction

Hey, kids!

As you grow up, you'll probably notice that a lot of things begin to change. You might have more responsibilities around the house or at school. Friendships start to change as you move away from being a kid to being a tween, and eventually, a teen. You may recently have started middle school, or you're getting ready to. All that change can be pretty scary, but it's okay! With the right life skills in your pocket, you'll be ready to tackle just about anything.

If you've read any of my other Life Skills books, you've already learned a lot, and if you haven't, don't worry! It's never too late to start learning. Out of all the skills I've talked about in the other books, the most important one to keep in mind as we work through this book is having a champion mindset.

Being a champion is all about resilience. It's about being able to face a challenge head-on, even if you don't get it right the first time. When you have a champion mindset, there's nothing you can't do. You're able to pick yourself up off the ground and keep working toward your goals.

Why? It's simple.

When you have a champion mindset, you know that if you keep practicing, you'll grow and get better at whatever you've set your mind to. Champions know that their success isn't based on what they can do right this minute—it's about what they can work on to do later, and how they can improve in the meantime.

If you can carry this mindset with you, you'll learn, grow, and succeed. As you succeed, you gain confidence. As you grow more confident, you know that you can keep moving forward when things get tough, and that'll be what guides you in the right direction.

Does that seem like too much? It shouldn't. You've been growing all along. You've learned to walk, talk, and read. You've learned to do math. You're still learning in school. You learn through practice, and that applies to everything in life.

You might not be an expert snowboarder today, but if that's something you love, you *could* be. You may not know how to play the guitar, but with enough practice, you could quickly learn. The people we look up to in life didn't start out knowing how to do everything perfectly. Even your parents were once children, learning how to walk, talk, and read. Now? They might look like they know it all, but they don't. They're learning every day too, just like you, and that never stops.

Champions know that learning is an ongoing process. They see mistakes and failures as opportunities to get better, so they keep working toward their goals. They practice consistently and they learn from their mistakes, so they can always improve. The best part? You can do this too!

As you read this book, remember what it means to have a champion mindset. When you struggle with some of the skills, remember that they'll get easier with time the more you practice them. You'll probably make mistakes from time to time, and that's okay! Mistakes just mean that you're still learning.

The skills in this book will help prepare you for your friendships, for setting up good habits that will help you succeed, and so much more. All you have to do is read it and start putting the tips and tricks to good use!

In the meantime, if you feel like anything is too hard or you don't understand something, remember that it's always okay to ask for help. The adults in your life love you and want you to grow and succeed, and they are some of your most valuable resources. Asking for help doesn't mean you have failed, either. It just means you need a little extra assistance, which is something we all need sometimes.

So, without further ado, let's dive in!

Chapter 1: Building Self-Discipline

When you're growing up, you face all sorts of challenges. From peer pressure to do something risky to impulsively making a decision that you regret later; it can be tough to get by sometimes. But, when you learn how to be self-disciplined, you can regain any and all control you may have lost.

Now, if your parents are like most, they probably tell you what to do. And if you're like most preteens, you likely feel that impulse to do the exact opposite thing of what they just said to do. Part of that is developing autonomy, which means that you want to be your own person and make your own decisions. It's normal to start feeling that urge to be yourself in the face of authority, but it's also a good idea to hear what your parents have to say at the same time.

Part of being able to fight that urge is to have the self-discipline to hear what authority figures say to you and understand what the right thing to do is. The other part is being able to put that understanding to the test and act accordingly.

Sometimes, this can be really hard because you want to do something, like ignoring your homework to play video games or chat with your bestie. Self-discipline can help with that too. That's why this chapter is here to give you the tools you need to start practicing it.

Self-Discipline and You

Self-discipline will help you in every area of your life. From making better friendships to being a better student, self-discipline is one of the biggest tools that will help you get there and is one of the key skills that successful adults use daily. It'll help you follow and achieve your goals and will also help you to stick to your values that matter the most.

If you're still a little confused about what self-discipline is, don't worry. It's not as complicated as it might sound. Self-discipline is a fancy way of saying that you are able to do things even if you don't want to do them. It gives you all sorts of benefits like:

- Feeling like you're in control of yourself

- Keeping sight of your goals so you can achieve them

- Building self-control and inner strength

- Having resilience

These might not sound important now, but when you're an adult and you're wholly responsible for your own actions, these will be lifesavers. Let's imagine a situation for a minute. You're an adult, and you've been looking forward to getting a treat all week long. You finally have time to go get it, and you walk into your favorite café, just in time to see the person in front of you buy the last brownie you've been dying to have all week.

You've got some options. You could trip them when they walk by so they don't get the brownie, either. You could argue with them about it and try pleading your case for that brownie. You could come up with some elaborate plot to steal it away from them. Or, you could have the self-discipline to not let your frustration and disappointment rule you.

Considering that when you're an adult, most of those options are strongly frowned upon, the smart, mature thing to do is to deal with your disappointment and move on with your day. Self-discipline will help you beat those impulsive thoughts and choose the mature action. After all, maturity is all about being in control of yourself.

Learning to Be Self-Disciplined

Being self-disciplined isn't always easy, but it is something you can practice. Remember that your brain is constantly growing and changing, and that means that you'll be able to learn new skills. The more you practice, the easier it will become, just like if you were to practice a sport.

Understand Your Strengths and Weaknesses

Part of being self-disciplined is being able to understand yourself. That includes your strengths and weaknesses. After all, you need to know what you can and can't do. For example, if you want to get into the habit of studying and doing your homework, you need to have a good idea of what will distract you and how you can keep yourself moving forward.

Maybe you get distracted by video games in your bedroom or by your friends when you try to do your homework together. These are weaknesses, and that's okay! Knowing that these are your weaknesses helps you to come up with good plans to move forward. You can choose to study somewhere that doesn't have video games or opt to do your homework before meeting up with your friends, so you know you won't be distracted.

On the other hand, knowing your strengths can help you too. If you know that you're good at learning with flashcards but bad at learning by just reading your textbook, you can use that to your advantage too.

Knowing what works best for you and what holds you back can help you to come up with the best strategies to help you succeed. It also gives you the clarity to choose what to avoid so you can make the choice to do so. The result? You'll be more productive!

Know What Keeps You Motivated

Another way to help yourself build self-discipline is knowing what keeps you motivated. All sorts of things can motivate you. You could, for example, be motivated by getting good grades, being liked, or earning rewards. You could also feel motivated when you listen to music that you really like or listen to someone who inspires you.

When we find what motivates us, it's easier to keep working toward our goals. Sometimes, the motivation might be something like avoiding a punishment or a bad result. Other times, it could be getting rewarded for what you've done. These are extrinsic motivators. Extrinsic means that they are external–they are outside of yourself.

Better motivators for self-discipline are intrinsic. Intrinsic motivation is the opposite of extrinsic. It's finding motivation from inside yourself. If you're motivated by feeling proud of yourself or by succeeding at something you've worked hard on, you're intrinsically motivated.

Both can be useful, but intrinsic motivation is what really drives us forward. We talk about intrinsic motivation as coming from the four C's. These are challenge, curiosity, control, and context.

- **Challenge:** Think of something that you love to do, even though it's hard. Maybe you really love karate or playing the piano. Even though it's hard and takes a lot of practice, you probably do it anyway. Think about how you feel when you do those things you love. Do you feel proud? Strong? Accomplished? Fulfilled? Those things you do for yourself reward you intrinsically because they challenge you and make you feel good.

- **Curiosity:** Sometimes, what motivates us is curiosity. Think of a time when you just had to learn more. Maybe you really like science and saw something interesting at a museum and had to keep researching it. Or, you could be curious about foreign languages or cooking. When you want to learn more, you're motivated by your desire to learn and grow as a person.

- **Control:** How does it feel when you lack control over a situation? Maybe it's having to follow your parents' rules or do homework assignments you really don't want to. It's probably not fun. Now, how does it feel when you *get* control over something? We usually feel good and motivated by being able to control ourselves and our environments. You might like taking control of what your bedroom looks like or what you do with your hair. Or, you might like taking control of your schedule. Choosing to do something on your own gives you that sense of control and the satisfaction that comes with it, which is useful for building self-discipline.

- **Context:** Context is all about the bigger picture. It's about seeing how something you're doing fits into the world at large. For example, seeing how being able to do math can help you with managing your budget or how learning to follow directions can help you cook delicious meals. Putting things in context can help motivate you by showing you how important it is to do or know something, which can help you stay self-disciplined enough to follow through.

So, what motivates you? Why do you do your homework or chores? Why do you do the things you love? Think about these things and figure out what it is that motivates you, so you can put them to use when it's time to do something you *don't* want to do.

Practice Consistency

When you're consistent about something, you do it reliably. You may consistently do your chores (regardless of reason) each day. You probably have a consistent bedtime and wake-up time for school. Consistency helps us to stay self-disciplined because it builds routine. Routines help us because they create predictability. We know what we're doing and when we're doing it. For example, you probably wake up and use the bathroom, then brush your teeth, eat breakfast, and get dressed for school. It's so consistent that you don't have to think about it—you just do it.

When there's something that you don't want or like to do that you have to get done, the best thing to do is make it consistent. Make it part of your regular routine. Do your homework at the same time each day, and it'll get easier to get done because you know you have to do it. The same goes for chores, extracurricular activities, or anything else you need to do.

Count Down Before You Start

If you're really having a hard time with consistency because you dread doing things you don't like, you can try counting down to your start time. I like this because it gives me a set time to prepare for something so I can jump in and get it done. Think of it like this: remember when your parents or teachers say that there are five minutes left before you're moving on to something else or you have ten minutes till lights out?

Try telling yourself that you're going to start doing something five minutes from now when you're feeling stuck and unmotivated. The most important part, though, is that you have to do it! No more excuses, waiting, or procrastinating. Just go. Less thinking, more action.

When in Doubt, Bribe Yourself

Yeah, yeah, I know. We just talked about how intrinsic motivation is best, but sometimes? It just doesn't work. Maybe you really, really, *REALLY* hate doing book reports. I don't blame you–I didn't like doing them either, and I turned out to be a writer! Sometimes, what works is to give yourself a reward for meeting your goals. I've seen kids who eat their favorite snack every time they read 20 pages of a book or complete their math homework. I've seen others who give themselves 15 minutes to play their favorite video game after studying for an hour.

Don't be afraid to give yourself a little boost by promising yourself a reward if you finish your task!

Chapter 2: How to Talk to Adults So They'll Listen

Being a kid is tough. It can feel like no one really listens to you or understands you when you speak. You can feel unheard, pushed aside, or uncared for, all because what you're trying to say doesn't seem to be sticking. First of all, don't be discouraged! Yes, it can be tough being your age, stuck in the in-between of being a kid and being a teenager. Some people may treat you like you're still younger than you are now, while others might expect you to act older, and it can be *confusing*.

Even worse, it can lead to communication failing.

Have you ever gone up to your parents or a teacher to talk to them about a problem, only for them to say something about you being dramatic? Or have you ever been told that something isn't nearly as big of a deal as you're making it? It can be frustrating, and if you're like me when I was your age, you probably feel like it's not worth bothering with. Why try to get help or confide in someone when they're just going to blow you off and make you feel like you don't matter?

First of all, what you have to say *does* matter. What also matters is *how* you say it. If you got a bad grade on your test and tried to tell your parents that *everyone* got bad grades and it's because the teacher sucks and you hate her, they may not be hearing the message that you really want to send. Yes, you're frustrated, and yes, you're speaking from emotion when you say these things, but is that really what the heart of the message you wanted to send is?

Sometimes, the best way to get an adult to listen is to know how to talk to them. And, I'm going to let you in on a little secret: talking to your parents doesn't have to be that different than talking to your friends. It needs honesty and sincerity. It also needs tact.

You're reaching a tough age, and I know how hard it can be to feel like your parents don't understand you, but with these tips and tricks, you can talk in a way that will help them get what you mean, and they may help you better understand your parents too.

Be Specific With What You Say

When it's time to chat with your parents about something important, like grades, issues with friends, or anything else that makes you nervous, the most important thing to do is be specific. Don't go into a long rant blaming everyone else for your problems when what you really mean to say is that you're upset about something.

Let's say that you forgot to finish a big project you had for English. Your grade was lowered because you had to turn it in late, and you just *know* that your parents will be upset about it. When you go to talk to them, don't give them a million excuses for why it's late. It's not the time to tell them how unfair it is that this teacher counts being late against your grade, or that the assignment was too long, or anything else. You want to be specific.

This means telling them that you *did* forget to turn in the assignment and that you know they'll be upset by your grade. Cutting straight to the point means that your parents hear exactly what you're trying to say.

On the other hand, maybe you did turn in your assignment on time, but you really didn't understand it. You might be feeling like you want to tell your parents all about how awful the teacher is and how he doesn't explain anything, and he assigns three times the homework any of your other teachers do. If you launch into your rant about these things, your parents may not take you as seriously as they would if you talked to them calmly about the issue at hand.

In this case, you might tell them, "I'm sorry, I tried my best, but I really just didn't get what the assignment was asking. I also think that the assignment was too much work, especially with all my other classes. Can you help me?"

Calm and to-the-point communication makes it easier for everyone involved to get on the same page, which also makes it easier to ask for help.

Don't Wait Until the Last Minute to Ask for Something

How often have you asked for something that you needed or wanted right away? Maybe it was asking to go out to the movies with your friends an hour before you were supposed to be there or realizing at 8:30 p.m. the night before a major project was due that you needed supplies from the store. When you wait until the last minute to talk to your parents, you'll probably get a no more often than not, which can be frustrating.

Some things are easier than others to ask in the moment, but for the big things, you should give your parents time to think and plan. You probably don't appreciate having things like chores sprung on you at the last minute, and your parents also probably won't appreciate being told they need to make a decision right that minute.

Plus, when you make it a point to give them extra time to consider what you've asked for, you show them respect. It tells your parents that it's something that you care about and you're giving them the time to give it all the consideration it deserves.

Choose the Right Time to Talk

It's not always the right time to approach a conversation with your parents, and if you try to, you're probably not going to get their full attention or consideration. For example, if you try to walk into your parents' home office while they're working because you want to talk about dying your hair, they're probably not going to be very pleased that you interrupted their work to ask about something that could have waited until later.

Be tactful with time. If your parents regularly drive you to or from school or to extracurricular activities, using the time you have in the car to talk together about things that matter to you can be a great way to open up conversations. Even better, when your parents are driving, you don't have to be face-to-face with them, which can sometimes make it even easier to talk about tough topics.

If you're not sure when a good time to talk is, make sure you ask them. Let them know that you'd like to have a conversation with them about something and ask them when a good time would be. Sometimes, they'll say that moment is perfect. Other times, they may ask you to put a pin in it until a little bit later. Either way, waiting until they can give you their full attention will go a long way.

Don't Get Defensive

When you communicate with your parents or other adults, it's easy to feel defensive. What they say or do can be frustrating and make you feel like you're not trusted. I get it! It's tough being asked where you're going, who you're talking to, or why you're doing something. Something to remember is that the adults in your life care about you. They're asking these questions because they want to make sure that everything is okay and that you're doing what you're supposed to be.

If you're hiding things from your parents, they probably have a feeling about it, and it's a good idea to be completely honest with them. They're there to help you, even if you've gotten yourself into a messy situation. If you're not, then there's nothing to be defensive about, and honesty is okay! When you're honest with them and doing what you're supposed to be, the truth gives them the chance to trust you.

You're growing up, and that means that you want privacy. You want trust and to be able to make your own decisions, and that's natural. Just remember that it's also natural for your parents to be worried about you and for them to want to check in with you too.

Tell Them What's Important to You

Things that are important to you may not be obvious to the adults in your life. Don't make them guess or expect them to just know. They can't read your mind any more than you can read theirs! Talking to the adults in your life about what's important to you and which things you enjoy is a great way for you to build trust and understanding between each other.

This is especially true if you notice that you and your parents disagree about something. Maybe they want you to quit something that you truly love because they think it's better for you to free up time for studies or meeting other obligations. If this happens, having a clear conversation about what matters to you and why it's so important can really bring clarity for everyone involved.

Make a list of your values and of what motivates you. Talk to them about these things, as well as what you enjoy and why. Doing so can help you find a way to find common ground. Your parents get the final say in what you do while you're still young, but that doesn't mean that you can't tell them what your priorities are.

You can even get your parents involved in what you like and what you care about. For example, you can share a book, music group, or activity to show them why you love it so much. They may be more open to understanding your side after you have.

Chapter 3: Being Self-Reliant

Has there ever been a time when you had to get something done entirely on your own or *wanted* to do on your own? Being self-reliant means that you can do and choose things for yourself. It's a normal part of growing up, and the skills you're learning in this book help you take a big step toward it.

Self-reliance is being able to handle your responsibilities and care on your own. When you're an adult, self-reliance is expected. When you move out into your own home, you'll have to handle your own chores, bills, and work without your parents there to handle every little thing.

That doesn't mean that you have to do it alone. You can always call for help if you need it, but being self-reliant helps you to learn to solve your problems without relying on someone else or their resources. You need to be able to stand on your own two feet, but you also need to know when it's right to ask for help with whatever you're trying to do.

What Is Self-Reliance?

Self-reliance can be kind of tough to understand fully, but there are several parts that go into it. For example, you need to have the ability to do something–remember when we talked about knowing your strengths and weaknesses? That plays a part here! You also need to be self-disciplined. A lot of these important skills for you to learn to be able to handle yourself are all linked together.

A lot of people break down self-reliance into needing five key skills:

Self-Motivation

Self-motivation is something we touched upon in the chapter on self-discipline. It's being able to find the intrinsic (internal) motivation to do something by yourself. Without it, you aren't really self-reliant, even if there are other external motivations to do something.

For example, let's say you want to get all of your assignments for the year done in advance so you have more free time later on. It's a great, worthy goal and is a step toward self-reliance if you can make sure you do it all on your own when you're supposed to! The problem is, if you don't feel an internal reason to do this, like feeling like it's good to get everything done in advance in case any problems arise, then you're probably not going to make very much progress.

Even if your parents put restrictions on things that you like to do until your homework is done, you're now relying on them to make sure that they're done, which isn't a form of self-reliance.

You need to find inspiration to do things on your own and learn to do them well. You probably have this for your favorite hobby, whether it's writing, drawing, singing, or playing sports. To be self-reliant, you have to do the same in other areas of your life too.

Self-Efficacy

Self-efficacy is a fancy way of saying that you believe in yourself and that you know that you can do something. You have to be able to trust yourself if you want to be self-reliant. You need to know your strengths and weaknesses and understand what you can and can't do.

If you're afraid that you can't do something, you might try to avoid it or pretend that it doesn't exist. This doesn't usually help a problem, but it does tend to make it worse, especially if you're afraid of asking for help. Part of being self-reliant is, after all, knowing what you can do!

It's okay to admit when you can't do something and need help. That doesn't mean that you're not generally a self-reliant person; it just means that you need help sometimes. We all do. Even doctors, who can help other people, still need to see doctors to help themselves.

You don't have to do it all, but you should do what you can without help. That's where self-efficacy comes in.

Instrumentality

Instrumentality is a big word that really just means having the means to an end. This is a fancy way of saying whether or not you can or can't do something right this moment. It kind of overlaps with self-efficacy in the sense that both question whether you can do something. Self-efficacy brings the added value of whether you trust yourself to do so.

When you have the instrumentality to do something, you've got the skills and tools you'll need. If you don't? You probably need to ask for help. Going back to the doctor example, a doctor might know what's wrong with them and know how to treat it, but if they need surgery done or if the treatment is somewhere they can't reach on their bodies, they're likely going to need to ask for help from someone. After all, a surgeon can't operate on themselves!

Another example could be money. You're at an age where you can do little odd jobs to make money, or you might get an allowance. You're not old enough to work a regular job, and that's okay. But that means that when you want to do something on your own that costs money or requires you to buy tools or supplies, you'll probably have to ask your parents for help.

Self-Direction

Self-direction is an aspect of self-discipline and self-motivation. It's being able to complete tasks on your own without relying on other people to keep you focused. Maybe you're trying to write a song or a book. If these are projects entirely for yourself, you need to be able to keep yourself focused on what matters. You don't have someone else telling you to write 500 words every day on your story or to work on your music.

When you have self-direction, you find ways to keep yourself accountable on your own. You set goals that help you to get to where you want to go. In previous books, I've talked about SMART goals, but they're worth reviewing. These are goals that you can complete that are:

- **Specific:** Specific goals are things that are clearly defined. For example, you want to train your dog to jump through hoops instead of saying you just want to train him.

- **Measurable:** Measurable goals have some way that you can judge your progress. For example, saying you want your dog to be able to jump through hoops at a certain height above the ground.

- **Achievable:** Achievable goals are goals that you can realistically do. For example, saying you want to save up money for a new phone when you're a babysitter for your neighbor and have money that comes in to you regularly.

- **Realistic:** Realistic goals are goals that you care about and *want* to achieve. For example, you want to learn how to play the piano because you care about it, not because your parents are making you.

- **Timely:** Timely goals are goals that can be put onto a schedule with milestones. For example, you have a goal to write 200 words a day on your big paper that's due next week, so you don't have to rush and get it done the night before.

SMART goals help you to find your self-direction because they outline ways that you can track your progress toward what you want to do. This is a powerful thing!

Self-Agency

Finally, self-reliance means that you have to have self-agency. Self-agency is the idea that you control yourself and your surroundings. It's the idea that you can make changes to your surroundings instead of waiting around to react to something else. When you have self-agency, you believe that you can choose your own fate and where you end up in the future.

This is all about trusting yourself to make good decisions and surrounding yourself with environments that will help you do so. Yes, this sounds a lot like self-discipline! They're related.

They're also related to that champion mindset I mentioned in the introduction. To have self-agency, you need to think of yourself as a learner. You need to see the world around you as flexible, as something that you can change to help you get to where you want to go in life.

For example, if you want to be an awesome lawyer as an adult, you need to go to law school. To go to law school, you have to go to college. To go to college, you have to do well in high school. To do well in high school, you need to learn the studying habits for success in middle school and elementary school. As cool as it would be to wake up one day as a lawyer, ready to go to court, that's not how the world works. If you want to be a lawyer, you have to make it happen. You have to make the choices now to work hard and study to take you to your end destination. That's self-agency.

Building Self-Reliance

So, how do all of the things we've just talked about turn into self-reliance? I'm going to be honest with you—it's a bit of work. It's easy to rely on other people to solve our problems or fix things for us, and it's easy to get into the habit of letting them do those things. The problem is, when you let other people do everything for you, you're not growing and learning.

Try on Your Own Before Asking for Help

You aren't expected to be entirely self-reliant. No one is. But you should be able to do many things for yourself. When you can, you should try to handle problems or things you need to do on your own. If you find that you can't, even after trying, then the next best thing is for you to ask for help. Know when you're stuck and see if someone else can teach you what you need to do or help you get out of the rut you're stuck in.

While you do this, don't be afraid of failing. Yes, it sucks to be stuck or see that even when you're trying your best, you're struggling. But, this is part of growing and developing that champion mindset. You'll be fine! Learn from that failure and ask for help.

Work on Problem Solving

Problem-solving skills are important to help you develop your own self-reliance. They're especially useful when you find yourself in a position where you fail at something and need to figure out how to not fail again in the future.

For example, if you got a bad grade on a test because you stayed up late to play games instead of studying, you've got a problem. Sure, your parents could take away your video games and make you study, but that's not really self-reliance, is it?

To be self-reliant, you'd need to solve the problem yourself, and this one has a pretty easy answer. Instead of staying up late playing video games, you can choose to study and then go to bed on time. It's boring, I know, but also a perfect way to solve your problem.

Your parents won't be able to take your video games away or ground you forever, so learning to make the right decisions now and how to solve your own problems will go a long way.

And often, the answer to solving the problem is as simple as looking to your self-discipline skills.

It Doesn't Have to Be Perfect

Are you a perfectionist? I know I am. I can sit and spend hours dreading doing something because I know it won't be exactly right. Maybe you're the same way, where anything less than being perfect is something that you consider a failure. This is a big problem a lot of the time because it leads to overthinking, and overthinking is one of the quickest ways to ruin your self-reliance.

When you overthink things, you spend too much time thinking about what you have to do and what can go wrong, and not enough time focused on what matters the most.

If you feel like you have to do something perfectly, then you probably don't trust yourself to get things done, which is going to stop you from being self-reliant. Remember that the most important thing is taking action and getting started. You can always make fixes afterwards, but it's important to get the ball rolling first and foremost.

Chapter 4: Staying Safe When Home Alone

Depending on your parents, maybe you've already stayed home alone, or maybe you're going to start being home alone soon. Either way, there are certain rules that are important to know so that you stay safe. Safety matters, and following the rules that your parents give you for staying home alone will go a long way in building trust with them! The more trust you build, the more likely they are to give you more freedom as you grow.

Staying home alone can be kind of scary for some kids at first. After all, you're used to having someone around who can take care of you and your needs. You're used to someone else being able to solve any problems that come up, like dropping a glass on the floor or if someone comes knocking at the door.

It's important to talk to your parents about these things before you stay home and understand their rules. What I'm talking about here will include general safety information, but your parents and their rules trump what you read in this book. Make sure that before you stay home alone, you and your parents are on the same page, and use these topics as conversations with your parents so you know how they want you to respond.

Staying Safe

One of the biggest parts of staying home alone is staying safe. Your parents want you to be safe and well, and the rules they set for you will help with that. When you stay home alone for the first time, you might think about all the freedom you have, but now isn't the time to start experimenting by skateboarding down the stairs or sliding down banisters! It's time to prove that you can handle such a big responsibility.

Follow All the Rules!

This is so important it needs to be reiterated! Your parents' rules for you are the number-one guidelines for staying safe at home. Follow their rules and ask permission if there's something you want to do that you're unsure about. You'll probably have some way to contact your parents or other adults while you're home alone, so don't be afraid to reach out to them when you're in doubt.

Make Sure Everything Is Locked

Doors and windows should all remain locked when you're home alone. Sure, it's not likely that anything will happen when your parents are away, but it's always better to be safe than sorry. When your parents leave, do a quick pass to make sure they're all shut and locked.

Be Careful with the Oven and Stove

If you have permission to cook in the oven and on the stove when your parents are away, make sure you're careful with them. It's easy to get burned or start a fire if you're not, and that's the last thing you want to do. Remember all of your safety training and make sure that when you're done with them, you turn them off all the way! This is especially important if your family uses gas appliances because if you don't turn the knobs back all the way to where they're supposed to be when they're off, they can leak gas into the house, and you might not notice it.

Know Where Your Phone is and Who to Contact in an Emergency

You should always have access to a phone when you're home alone for safety reasons. Make sure that you keep it charged, and don't forget to answer when your parents call or text you. Even if you normally leave your phone on vibrate or silent, this is a good time to turn the volume all the way up so you'll hear it if you leave it in another room—which you shouldn't do!

Make sure that you and your parents also discuss who you can contact if there's something wrong and you can't get a hold of them. Sometimes, things can happen, and your parents won't be able to answer you right away, depending on why they left you home alone. Knowing which neighbors, friends, or family members you can contact helps give you peace of mind because you'll know exactly who to call for help if you need it.

Don't Answer the Door to Strangers

This seems pretty self-explanatory, but if you're home alone and a stranger comes knocking, you shouldn't answer the door. Even if it looks like they're a professional or they say that they just want to talk to you for a minute, keep it shut and call your parents for guidance on what to do. If they were expecting somebody to stop by, they probably would have told you!

Handling Unexpected Events

Sometimes, unexpected things happen. We can't know if or when they'll happen, but we can plan accordingly. When you know how to handle unexpected events like a fire, a water line breaking, or a big storm, you'll be more prepared, and they'll feel much less scary.

Know How to Turn Off the Water Supply

Do you know where the water supply to your house or apartment is? Houses and most apartments will have a knob that you can twist somewhere to cut off all the water to the inside. This might seem like a bad idea, but sometimes, you have to do it.

If there's a break in a line or if you can't get water to stop coming from a toilet, sink, or tub, you may need to turn off the water supply. This will stop any more water from coming through and flooding your home, which protects it and your belongings from damage. Before you stay home alone, ask your parents where the water supply is and have them show you how to use it so you're prepared.

Know Where Flashlights and Other Supplies Are in Case of a Power Outage

Power outages can happen unexpectedly, whether due to a storm knocking down power lines, a transformer breaking, or just because something went wrong in your house. While this doesn't usually matter during the daytime, at night, it can be scary.

Your parents probably have a kit for power outages to help in these situations. It probably has candles or flashlights, as well as possibly warm blankets if it happens in the winter and cuts off your access to heat. Talk to your parents about where these emergency supplies are kept and what you should do if the power goes out.

Know How to Flip a Circuit

If the power goes out to only one part of your home or to only a few appliances, there's a good chance that the breaker flipped and needs to be reset. Once you reset the breaker, the power should be restored. Ask your parents where the circuit panel in your home is. It'll be a big metal box on a wall or in your garage.

Once you know where it is, it's usually as simple as looking for the switch that has moved from the on position to the off position, and you'll have to flip it back to on. If it's halfway between positions, switch it off first, then turn it back on. If this doesn't work or if the breaker shuts off again, your home may have other problems that need to be addressed, and you should report it to your parents as soon as possible.

Brush Up on Fire Safety

When was the last time you went through your fire safety information? Do you know where you need to go if there's a big fire? Do you know where the fire extinguisher is if it's a small one? These are important things to know because if a fire starts, every second counts. You need to know where these things are and how to use the fire extinguisher your family has.

If a fire starts when you're cooking, there's a good chance it's a grease fire, and you might feel like the best answer is to throw water on it to put it out. Don't do this! This is a surefire way to make the oil explode, and it can hurt you and spread the fire. Have you ever seen a frying pan with hot oil have water drop into it? It sputters and spits out scalding hot oil. When you throw a whole lot of water on it to try to put it out, that happens, but on a much bigger scale. It's no good!

If the fire is in the oven, turn it off and keep the oven door closed. Don't open it up and try to handle it yourself, especially if you have a gas range. Ideally, with the door shut, the fire will run out of oxygen and die off (if you didn't know, fire cannot stay alive if there is no oxygen!) If it doesn't, and smoke keeps coming from it, or if there are large flames coming from it, call the fire department for help.

If you start a fire in a pan or on your stove, you can't always suffocate the fire out as easily. Make sure you turn off the stove before you do anything else. You could try putting an oven mitt on and putting a metal lid on the pan that's on fire to stop the flames, but only if it's safe.

Don't put a glass lid on since it could shatter and make an even more dangerous mess. If you don't have a metal lid, you could try putting a metal baking sheet over it instead. If you can't do this because the flames are too high, don't try; instead, use a fire extinguisher. Small grease fires can be put out with baking soda or salt as well, but it's better to try to smother the fire with a lid or use a fire extinguisher.

If the fire doesn't go out or is too big for you to handle safely, go outside and call 911 so that the fire department is notified. They'll be able to come and put out the fire.

Brush Up on Emergency Safety

This tip will depend on where you live. Do you get earthquakes in your area? Tornadoes? Giant thunderstorms? Wildfires? You and your family should have plans for any natural disasters that might happen in your area. Before you stay home alone, pick a time to brush up on what's expected of you if one of these happens unexpectedly. Talk to your parents about what you should do in these situations if you're home alone.

Chapter 5: Managing Big Emotions and Mood Swings

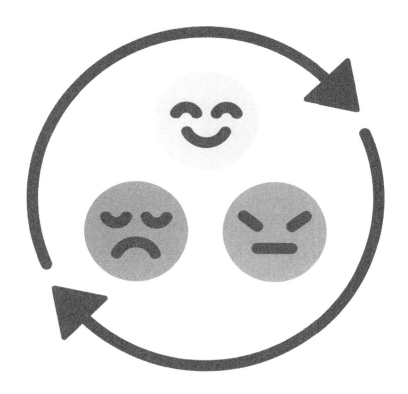

As you're growing up, it's normal to go through mood swings. At 11, your body is probably beginning to change and go through puberty. This means that your body is producing hormones that will help it change from being a biologically immature child to being a mature adult who is capable of reproduction. Unfortunately, this comes with a whole slew of changes.

Before we get into these changes, let's explain what a hormone is.

You know how when you play a video game, you press buttons to make the characters move or do actions? Your body has a similar system, but instead of buttons and video game characters, it uses things called hormones.

Hormones are like tiny messengers in your body. They travel through your bloodstream to different parts of your body and give instructions. For example, when you're running a race and you feel your heart beating faster, that's because a hormone told it to do so. Or when you start growing taller, that's because a hormone gave the instruction to your body to grow.

So, hormones are kind of like the body's video game controller, helping to control different parts of your body and what they do.

As you go through puberty, acne, body odor, and body hair may all pop up during this time as your body matures. Unfortunately, all those hormones flowing through your body can also create some pretty big moods and mood swings. These emotions can vary from being really upset about something, feeling like no one understands you, or even making you take a special interest in another person as you develop crushes.

These big emotions can be tough to deal with. They might even feel like they're controlling you, and you feel like you regret what you did because of them later on. It's okay to have big feelings, but it's not always okay to act upon them. While you may not be able to prevent yourself from feeling a certain way, you can control what you do with these feelings.

What's Happening to Your Body?

As puberty happens, a part of your brain called the hypothalamus releases a hormone with a big name called gonadotropin-releasing hormone, which can be shortened to GnRH. GnRH goes from your hypothalamus to your pituitary glands, which triggers it to release two different hormones with names that are also a mouthful to say–luteinizing hormone and follicle-stimulating hormone. These hormones then tell your ovaries or testes to release estrogen and testosterone, which is what then changes your body. If these words are confusing right now, don't worry, you will learn them in school soon.

This process usually happens to boys sometime between the ages of 9 and 14 and to girls between the ages of 8 and 13. Maybe it's already happened to you, or it'll happen soon. You'll notice your body growing quicker than it did before. Boys may notice their voices change, and girls may start menstruating during this period. Your body will also go through several other changes as it grows into an adult.

As your body changes, you'll probably have lots of questions for your doctor or parents, and that's okay! Even if you feel like they don't understand, remember that they went through puberty, too, mood swings, voice cracks and all!

Mood Swings and Puberty

All those hormones that help your body grow can also cause mood swings. You might be happy one minute but anxious the next. It can be scary to suddenly feel these giant changes in emotions, but there's nothing wrong with you. Your body is just growing up, and growing up means change, but change isn't a bad thing. Now's the time to start working on skills to control your emotions and get used to the new you before you're an adult, and your parents are the best guides during this time.

Some of the best ways to control those mood swings are taking care of yourself and finding ways to make you feel better and more grounded in yourself.

Don't Bottle Your Feelings!

Most importantly, make sure you don't bottle up your feelings, no matter what they are. When you try to ignore and bottle them, all you're doing is adding pressure on yourself. Think of yourself as a bottle of soda. Every time you get upset about something, imagine that you've been shaken up. When you shake a bottle of soda, you build pressure inside of it because of all the carbon dioxide mixed into it. What happens when you finally open a bottle that's been shaken up?

It explodes!

People work the same way. When we bottle up our emotions, we don't let off steam (or carbon dioxide, using the soda example), and eventually, the bottle will be opened. If you've pushed down all those feelings, what'll happen is that they'll all blow up and make a much bigger mess of things than if you'd dealt with them as they arose.

Get Moving!

Exercise is good for more than just your body. It's also good for your mind. When you exercise, you can let go of the stress you feel by putting it to good use elsewhere. Maybe you like to play sports. This can be a great outlet for those big moods that you feel and give you a safe space to be competitive with friends or peers.

If you don't like sports, there are other ways to get moving too. Anything that gets your blood pumping counts! Go for a walk, play with your dog, dance to your favorite music, or find anything else that you enjoy that requires you to move. You'll probably feel better after!

Sleep On Time

When you don't get enough sleep, your body is under stress, which can really mess with your mood. It can be hard to get the right amount of sleep when you're busy with school, friends, and everything else you do during the day, but it's vital for you. Protect your sleep schedule, even if it seems uncool or there's something else you'd rather do.

Eat Healthy Foods

Healthy foods can also help you feel better emotionally. Your mind and your digestive system are linked together by something called the gut-brain axis. When you eat healthy foods and have healthy bacteria in your digestive system, your brain can produce hormones that are good for mood regulation, meaning that you'll feel much better.

Stay Engaged with Friends

One of the best ways to get rid of big feelings is to talk about them with someone. During puberty, you might start feeling as if you don't belong or that you don't deserve to have good friends. All these changes can really make it hard to connect with your friends and make sure that you're happy.

Good friends are supportive and are there for you when you need to vent about what's going on in your life. They'll be there to talk to when you need them the most. Just make sure you return the favor for them, too!

When you're feeling really strong emotions about something, your friends may understand where you're coming from better than your parents or other adults in your life. They're probably in the same spot you are, dealing with big moods as they grow too.

Do What You Love

Spending some time doing what you love, especially if it's creative, can be a great emotional outlet. Maybe you draw something that represents your current mood, or you listen to music that really resonates with you. These are great ways to go through catharsis. Catharsis is the process through which you release strong emotions and feel better.

So put away time for yourself to pursue your hobbies and enjoy yourself, especially when you're in a particularly bad funk. It'll help a ton!

Don't Be Afraid to Take a Break

If you're doing something and get frustrated with it, it's okay to step away before your feelings get out of control. Even adults need this sometimes. Have your parents ever looked at you and said, "We'll talk about this later," after they've gotten upset about something you've done? That's taking a break! It's a very healthy way to deal with strong negative emotions because it gives you time to let the strong feelings pass before addressing the problem.

Burn Letters and Journaling

Writing down what you're feeling is another great way you can get all those negative feelings out. Writing them down on paper or on your computer is also a good way to get insight into what's bothering you. When you write down your feelings and why you have them, you can start seeing patterns, or you might get to a solution that you otherwise wouldn't have seen.

When I was younger, I also really liked writing burn letters. You don't actually have to burn them, but the point of them is to vent out all of your feelings and then never actually give them to the intended recipient. Write out all of your complaints and problems you have with someone and get it all out. It doesn't matter what you write, even if it's insulting or mean, since you won't be giving the letter to the person you're writing to. When you're done, read over everything, contemplate upon it, then crumple up the letter and throw it away.

Chapter 6: Studying Well

Studying is usually never fun, but it is something that you'll need to do. As you enter middle and, eventually, high school, you'll have much more to do than you did in elementary school. You have more classes that you're taking, and that means more opportunities for homework, tests, and projects that need to be completed.

If you have dreams of going to college or becoming a high-performance person one day, the best thing you can do is set good studying habits now so you'll be prepared for when it gets harder. The good news here is that some of the skills we've already been talking about in the book so far all lead up to this one.

You'll need self-discipline and self-reliance if you want to be a successful student. And, if you're one of those students who already gets good grades with very little effort, you'll still want to put these skills to good use. I get it — why spend more time on something than you need to? Well, the answer is simple. Right now, school is easier than it'll ever be again in the future. High school is harder and more demanding than middle school. College is even more demanding than that. You don't want to get to college and realize that you have no idea how to study well and work toward getting good grades.

This chapter is all about setting up good studying habits that will help you in school now, and in the future. The sooner that you make a good habit out of studying, the easier it'll be in the future.

Stay Organized

Organization is your best friend when you start taking more classes. In middle school, you probably have your four core classes of science, social studies, language arts, and math. You also probably have two or more elective classes, like foreign languages, art, or music. All of these will have different supplies, assignments, and papers to keep track of. That's why you need to stay organized – when you know where everything is and what you need to do, you won't be scrambling to finish things last minute.

Keep a Planner

A planner is like a calendar book where you can write down all your assignments. You might think that you can just memorize what you need to do, and if you don't have much, that's probably true, but keeping a planner is a good habit to build. Even if you only have to write down a few things on some days, get into the habit of writing down all assignments and due dates in one spot so you'll always know what you need to do.

Keep a Schedule

Staying organized is also about keeping a general schedule so you know that you always have a set time to get your work done. Maybe you get home from school and take a short break for a snack. Then, you can set up a schedule for the order you'll do your homework in. You might practice the saxophone from 4 p.m. to 4:20 p.m., then do your 20 minutes of reading for language arts, then work on math homework starting at 4:40 p.m., for example.

Make a schedule that makes sense for you and your obligations. It'll help you to stay on top of things.

Keep Your Supplies Organized

Does your backpack have any sort of organization to it? Or are you the kind of kid that just shoves everything in haphazardly and hope that you can find your assignment when you get home?

Set up some sort of organization where you use folders or binders to keep track of your classwork. Ideally, you'll have folders or dividers for each class so you can keep up with it all.

Choose a Dedicated Study Space

Where you study matters just as much as how you study. When you set a space to be dedicated to studying, you make it a habit to do your homework when you're in that spot. Maybe it's a desk in your bedroom, or a home office, or your dining table or kitchen island. Wherever it is, make sure that you can work without distractions. Some people have luck studying at the library because it's quiet. This could be an option for you, too, if you live near one.

Cut out all the distractions too. If you're studying, you shouldn't be chatting on social media, playing video games, or watching TV. If you need music on, it should be something that's relaxing and not distracting, like genres that don't have lyrics.

Make a Studying Plan

Part of effective studying is having a plan that's realistic. Do you do well in math? Do you struggle with language arts? Plan your time accordingly. If you have subjects that you're strong in, you probably don't need to spend as much time on them as you do on ones that are harder for you. Set up a weekly plan with your assignments to give each subject the time you need to learn the material. The key here is to plan your time in advance so you don't find yourself scrambling last minute to get projects done.

Learn How to Take Notes

As you go into middle school, you'll probably have to take more notes than you did before. And in high school and college, these notes will be even more detailed. Learn how to take notes on important information and focus on what matters.

If your teacher uses slides in class with information, you probably want to write down what's on them, as well as notes about what's being discussed. If you're reading for an assignment, take notes on important details.

Taking notes is about more than just studying them later. Often, writing down information can help you remember it better too. Studies show that writing by hand is often more effective. You'll want to write down vocabulary words and concepts that your teacher is presenting, as well as examples when you can.

Figure Out Your Learning Style

We all learn differently, and knowing how you learn can help make your studying habits more useful to you. Most people learn through one of three categories. These are visual, auditory, and kinesthetic.

Visual Learners

Visual learners do best with having information in front of them. They like images, diagrams, and graphic organizers to see how things work together. You may do best as a visual learner if you color code your notes or use symbols. For example, you might use an exclamation point next to important information or a question mark if you need to keep working on it.

Flashcards can also be a useful tool for a visual learner, especially if you're learning concepts, key terms, or vocabulary.

Outlines work well for visual learners, mixing headings, subheadings, and bullet points into your notes. For example, let's say you're taking notes about how plants grow. You might have something that looks like this:

Plant Life Cycle:

- **Seed**
  - Seeds need to germinate to sprout.
  - Requires being planted in soil with water and sun.
  - Seed will crack open with a root and begin to sprout.

- **Sprout**
  - Sprouts have roots growing into the ground and stems growing toward the light source.
  - Sprouts have immature leaves.

- **Small Plant**
  - Small plants begin to grow mature leaves.
  - Plants use photosynthesis to grow.

- Photosynthesis uses sunlight to create sugar from water and carbon dioxide.
- Sugar gives the plants energy.

- **Adult Plant**
  - Adult plants reproduce with flowers, fruits, and seeds.

This is a quick outline that gives you all the information you'd need to know. You can make outlines like this for nearly any subject.

Auditory Learners

Auditory learners do best when they hear or speak the material. They do best with group discussions or lectures. If you're an auditory learner, reading the material out loud when you study could be one of the best ways to really get the information to stick.

One tip for auditory learners is the use of mnemonic devices. These are tools that help you to remember things. Think of how you may have heard Never Eat Soggy Waffles or Never Eat

Sour Watermelon when learning the directions on a map. You know that the directions go clockwise on a compass rose, with north pointing up to the top. When you remember Never Eat Soggy Waffles, you know that going around the map, you'll start with the point facing up as north, then the one facing right as east, the one facing down as south, and the one facing left as west.

Other common mnemonic devices you've probably encountered are:

- BEDMAS for remembering the order of operations: brackets, exponents, division and multiplication, addition and subtraction.

- "Righty tighty, lefty loosey" when trying to screw or unscrew something.

- "My Very Educated Mother Just Served Us Nachos" for remembering the order of the planets: Mercury, Venus, Earth, Mars, Jupiter, Saturn, Uranus, Neptune.

When you're studying, come up with some for yourself to help you remember the material.

Kinesthetic Learners

Kinesthetic learners are people who learn through hands-on methods. They may, for example, learn how to do math by actively *doing* it rather than studying notes. They may be particularly strong at science because they get to do experiments that help them to learn.

Kinesthetic learners may have issues with school because so much of it is about reading and writing, which isn't always the best option for them. If you learn like this, there are ways that you can make it easier for yourself. Try some of these tips to see if they help:

- Be active while studying. You can walk or pace with your textbook or notes.

- Type your notes. Using a keyboard can help you to remember the information better, even though most people learn better writing by hand.

- Play with a fidget spinner or similar toy while reading your notes.

- Use your finger to guide your reading.

- Use a finger in the air to write out your notes as you envision them in your mind.

One important thing to note is that you may not exclusively be any one of these 3 learning types. Most people, including myself, are a mix of all 3, so you may learn best by incorporating techniques from all 3 categories.

Chapter 7: Caring for Yourself When You're Sick

No one likes feeling under the weather. Sure, you have your parents around to help you feel better now, but what if they have to go to work and you stay home alone? What about when you're older and living in a college dorm without them? Learning how to care for yourself when you're sick now means that by the time you'll have to do it out of necessity, you'll already be well-prepared for it.

Really, caring for yourself is all about making sure that you stay healthy and give your body plenty of time to rest. We all get colds from time to time, and it's never fun, but your body is meant to fight off those infections and help you feel better in no time. Even if you feel like garbage today, in a few days, you'll probably feel worlds better if you take the time to give your body what it needs the most, which is rest.

Stay Home and Rest When You Need It

When you get a cold, the symptoms often come out of nowhere. You might go to sleep feeling great and wake up feeling down in the dumps. Sometimes, you might feel well enough to go to school, but when your whole body aches and you feel like you could sleep for a lifetime, the best thing you can do is rest.

Not only will the rest help your body conserve energy to use for fighting off the cold, but this will also prevent you from spreading germs to other people and infecting them. If all you have is a case of the sniffles with a sore throat, you're probably okay to keep up with your daily tasks, as long as you take precautions not to infect other people. But if you have a fever or chills and feel tired, you probably want to take that time to rest for a few days instead.

Don't Forget to Hydrate

When your throat hurts, it can be tough to drink anything. The same goes if you're vomiting or have diarrhea. But, when you're sick, being hydrated is even more important than when you're well. Staying hydrated helps your respiratory system thin mucus that can cause you to feel congested. It also helps to decrease irritation in your throat and nose when you cough or sneeze.

Make sure you're drinking plenty of water, warm teas, or broths to help yourself recover. When you get dehydrated, your blood is more concentrated than it would be otherwise because the plasma that your blood floats in is mostly water. Without that water, your body has to work harder to function, which means less energy for your immune system to fend off the infection.

Use Humidity for Congestion

If you're feeling particularly gunked up, it can be tough to breathe. Your nose might be all clogged up, and you find yourself coughing a lot. When this happens, the best trick is to go for humidity. You can use a humidifier in the room you're in, or if you don't have one, you can sit in a nice, steamy shower for a while. It will help thin out all the mucus that is making you feel clogged up.

Treat the Symptoms

Now, this is one that you'll probably need some parental help with because it involves medicine. If you have a high fever, you probably need medicine to bring it down a bit. Fevers are important because they help your immune system work more efficiently and make an unwelcoming environment for whatever bacteria or virus is making you sick. But when fevers get too high, they can be dangerous.

Take your temperature regularly, and if you notice that you have a fever, you should talk to your parents about it. They may offer you some cold medicine to help you feel better. This can also help to stop aches and pains if you have them.

Other medicine can be useful for slowing vomiting or diarrhea if you have a stomach bug. These medicines soothe the stomach and may help you to keep down important fluids or food that you need.

Keep Up with Hygiene

When you're sick, it can be hard to do just about anything. You might just not have the energy to do much more than sit in bed, and that's okay. One thing you should keep in mind when you're sick, though, is that you don't want to get everyone else around you sick too. You should wash your hands regularly, especially before touching things that everyone else in your home touches.

Once you're feeling better, there are some steps you can take to help keep everyone else well, too, like making sure you or a parent sanitizes your room's surfaces and washing your bedding or any clothes that you wore while sick. This helps to get rid of anything left behind by your cold that might infect someone else.

Ask For Help!

While it's good to be self-reliant and take care of yourself when you're not feeling well, you also shouldn't be afraid to ask for help if you need it. If you notice that you're feeling really unwell, or it's hard to breathe, you should talk to your parents. You should also ask them for help if you have a cold that isn't going away. It's possible you might need to be seen by a doctor to get antibiotics or other medicine to help your body fight off the infection.

Chapter 8: Loving Yourself

When you look into a mirror, what do you see? So much of how we see ourselves comes from how we think other people see us. If you look at yourself and see anything less than a strong, beautiful, unique person capable of taking on the world and handling anything thrown your way, you might be a bit too harsh on yourself. You should be your biggest cheerleader, and if you don't think you deserve the cheerleading, then you may not love yourself like you should.

Loving yourself isn't selfish or self-centered. It's about seeing yourself for who you are: Someone deserving of love, compassion, respect, and friendship. You, like everyone else in this world, matter.

It doesn't matter what you look like, what your interests are, or how you dress yourself. You matter. You deserve love. And you should love yourself for who you are.

Accepting yourself as who you are and loving yourself for being who you are will help you to build confidence that will also take you to great places. Remember, part of having that champion mindset is to accept yourself and grow as a person from that, not to hold yourself back.

Loving yourself can be loving how you look, even as your body starts to change. It can be taking care of your body by feeding it well and exercising regularly. It can also be giving yourself time to enjoy yourself and the things you love to do.

Body Positivity and Loving Yourself

As your body changes, you might find yourself comparing what you look like to what other people look like. Maybe you wish you had more muscle, or you wish that you had less of a tummy. You might not like that you get acne or you're growing more hair than you used to in places that you didn't have it before.

Your body is your own, and it's the only one you've got. There's no use in comparing it to other people's because you aren't them. Your body is as unique as your fingerprint and your DNA, and it's special just for you. Even if it doesn't look exactly how you'd like it to, you should still accept it for what it is and only try to change the things that you can actively control.

Don't Be Negative About Your Body

If you look in the mirror and find yourself criticizing every little thing you see, it's time to stop. Your body may not look like the pictures you see in magazines or at the movies, and that's okay. It doesn't have to, and right now, it's still growing and changing. What you look like now and what you'll look like when you're older are two completely different things, and that's okay!

When you start saying negative things about yourself, or criticizing how you look, remember to stop and take a step back. Those negative thoughts aren't going to do anything but make you feel bad about yourself, and that's not going to help you with anything.

Look in the Mirror and Say Three Kind Things to Yourself

Instead, when you find yourself getting stuck in that rut of saying negative things about yourself, try reframing your thoughts. Look in the mirror and give yourself three kind compliments. Maybe you really like your eye color, or maybe your hair looks good today. You could say that your outfit looks great on you or that you can see how you're getting stronger or taller.

Switching to saying kind things about yourself instead of negative things helps you to paint yourself in a different light. If there are things about how you look that you don't like, try to think about them from a neutral perspective instead. This means that you don't say anything positive, but you also don't say anything negative either.

Work on Self-Care

Even when there are things you don't like about how you look, you can still practice self-care. Exercising, sleeping well, eating healthy foods, and staying hydrated all help your body to be its healthiest. Take care of your body by keeping it clean and well-kept. These can go a long way to help you feel better about it if you don't like it.

Loving Who You Are

You are more than just your body. You're also your personality, and that deserves to be loved and accepted too. You are worthy of love from yourself and from others, but sometimes, people have a hard time respecting people who don't respect themselves. It's not right, but it is something that happens. By loving who you are as a person, you can build self-confidence, and often, self-confidence is what makes us the most attractive. It's what makes us a good friend and fun to be around.

Accept Yourself and Your Interests

Do you have interests that other people laugh at? Maybe you really like chess or anime or something else that isn't as popular as other things, and you're afraid you'll be teased for it. This can make you feel like you have to hide yourself and your true values.

You and your interests are valid. It doesn't matter what other people think about what you do in your free time, and you shouldn't feel ashamed of your hobbies and special interests. The people who shame or bully you for them are wrong.

When you accept your own interests, you can start finding people who relate to you and share similar ones to yourself. This is also a great way for you to make new friends with your shared values. You don't have to follow the main path to be happy or have friends. You just have to be yourself, and that means accepting who you are as a person.

Celebrate Your Wins

When you're feeling down on yourself, sometimes, looking at the positives is a good way to get yourself out of your funk. Instead of looking at the times you got something wrong, focus on ways that you've succeeded. These could be times you got good grades in school or when you were able to beat a previous record at a sport. You've done things in life worth celebrating before, so by not letting those be shrouded by what you've gotten wrong, you can feel much better about yourself.

Make a list of all the things you're proud of doing recently. You'd be surprised at what's on there and how many things you've done that are worth celebrating and deserving of praise.

Chapter 9: Speaking in Front of a Group

One of the most practical life skills you'll need is public speaking. It's something that you'll probably need with presentations and maybe even at jobs in the future. For some people, this comes easily. For others, it's one of the worst things in the world. And I totally get it – I don't like standing in front of an audience, either.

However, learning to speak publicly helps you develop better communication skills and can also help you feel more confident. It can give you a chance to plan out a presentation and figure out ways to organize your thoughts, and it also helps you to develop important leadership skills that you'll need later in life.

Unfortunately, it also means putting yourself in the public eye, surrounded by your peers who are all watching your every movement. That's a lot of pressure for one kid to take! Growing up, I hated giving presentations because they always made me nervous. I was pretty shy in middle school, and having to speak in front of a crowd was enough to send chills down my spine and put butterflies in my stomach. I had to get over it, but I still hate speaking in front of a crowd. It's a lot easier now but still intimidating.

Prepare in Advance

The best thing you can do when you know you'll have to speak in front of a crowd is to prepare in advance. This means outlining what you want to say, planning how you'll say it, and practicing your presentation in advance. You might want to ask a friend or family member to listen to your presentation so they can give you feedback on how you handle it.

The more that you practice your presentation, the easier it gets when you go in front of a crowd because you already know what you're going to say. The more prepared you are, the better. You might want to consider taking notes on notecards to help you remember the most important parts of your presentation too.

Recording yourself can also help you prepare for your presentation because when you do, you're able to listen back to what you've said. This helps you to figure out any points that are tough for you, which you can work out in advance.

Be Confident

Confidence is the key to a lot in life, and it's one of the biggest keys when you have to speak in front of a group for any reason. When you're nervous and timid, your body language and voice give you away. People can tell that you're not feeling very confident, and that can make your presentation less successful because they won't pay as much attention to you.

Confidence takes time to build, but many of the skills we've been talking about throughout the book will help you with that. Remember that champion mindset, too – when you mess something up, it's just another opportunity for growth and improvement! When you have to speak to a group, make sure you keep your voice clear and loud enough for everyone to hear. It's not the time to mumble!

You'll also want to make sure you keep your body language open and approachable. This means that you'll keep your arms uncrossed and your hands visible. Don't fidget or mess with your hair and try to make eye contact as you speak. If eye contact is too stressful for you, you can also look right between people's eyes, and they'll think you're making eye contact with them, and that can help them think you're more confident than you actually feel.

Prepare for the Worst

What's the worst thing that can happen when you give a speech or presentation? Maybe you're afraid of saying the wrong word, or you worry that you'll drop your notes or suffer a major wardrobe malfunction.

To help put those worries at ease, you can think about everything that could go wrong and then plan out what you'd do if that actually happened. For example, if you're afraid your hair will spontaneously combust, you could tell yourself that you'll stop, drop, and roll. If you're afraid you'll say the wrong word, you can remind yourself that we all say the wrong thing sometimes and that all you have to do is correct the word and move on.

Sometimes, planning out what you'd do, even in the most far-fetched of situations, can give you the peace of mind you need to do better. After all, when you have a plan, you have nothing to really worry about, right?

When in Doubt, Imagine Everyone in Their Underwear

If all else fails, you can make yourself feel better by imagining that your audience is all only wearing their underwear or in some other embarrassing situation. Maybe you imagine them all wearing funny hats or with silly mustaches drawn on their faces with permanent marker.

The point of this is to make your audience seem less intimidating. When they're not so threatening or intimidating to you, it's easier to get the words out.

Chapter 10: Being Adaptable

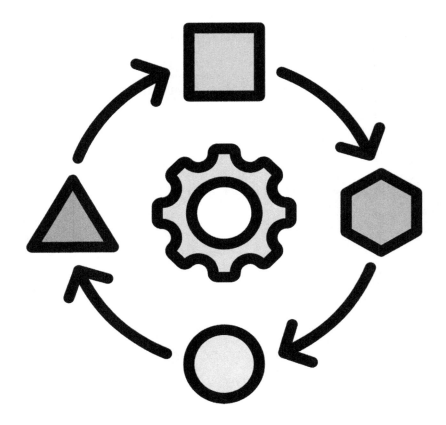

Have you ever been working on a project when suddenly, everything just goes wrong? Or maybe you were playing a game and doing really well, but out of nowhere, the opponent suddenly overtakes your score, and you're going to lose. It can be frustrating! When you've been working hard for something, only to have it crumble away. You may feel like giving up, but that's not the right choice.

Remember, champions never give up! Even when something goes wrong, there are ways that you can continue learning and working toward your goal.

One of the things you can do is learn to be adaptable. To be adaptable is to be able to change what you're doing based on what's going on around you, especially when something goes wrong or not according to plan.

Learning to be adaptable now will help you to better cope in the future if something goes wrong. It'll teach you how to better deal with unexpected situations, which is something you'll face a lot in the future as you get older. So, how do you learn to be adaptable? It's not as hard as you'd think, but if you're the kind of person that has rigid rules that you like to follow, you'll have to push yourself out of your comfort zone a bit.

Change Things Up

If you have a routine that you follow, it's pretty easy to feel upset when it doesn't go exactly according to plan. After all, routine is comfortable and predictable. We know exactly what will happen and when. Unfortunately, life doesn't work on routines alone. While they're helpful tools, they also can change unexpectedly, like if there's an accident, if someone gets sick, or if something just breaks.

Think about a time your routine has fallen apart. Maybe you were working on your homework, but the windstorm knocked the power out. Now what? Well, you've got some options, depending on the situation. You could choose to give up, mope, and not bother trying to do your homework, which your teacher probably won't appreciate. Or, you could take action by being adaptable. For example, you could find a way that you could study without power, such as using a flashlight to read your book and take notes instead.

What can help you prepare for those moments when life is unpredictable is to mix up your routine on purpose sometimes. Maybe this already happens based on your parents' and family's responsibilities, such as if you have to go with your parents to a sibling's ball game or a recital. Or, you could decide to volunteer and go out of your way to mix things up another way. Teaching yourself to deal with changes to your routine from time to time prepares you to handle it when your routine changes on its own.

Don't Be Afraid of Failure, Learn From It

Sometimes, what holds us back is failure. It's seeing that something completely falls apart, even though we were doing what we always did. In these cases, failure is valuable – it's a learning tool. Part of being adaptable is being able to pick yourself back up, dust off your knees, and get right back into the thick of things, knowing that you can always try something else.

For example, if you got a problem wrong on a math test, you could always try redoing it with a different strategy. If you're trying to write a code for a game you like to play and it doesn't quite work out the first time, you wouldn't go back through and write the exact same code a second time, would you? No! You'd come up with a different way to try to get what you want. When you fail, take it as practice in being adaptable and flexible. Try again with a different method to see if you get a different result. If you still fail, then try again a different way until you find the right one.

Try New Things

When was the last time you tried something new? How did it go? Pushing ourselves out of our comfort zones and trying something new can be intimidating, but it's also important. After all, if we never try anything new, how can we grow? How will you know if you like or dislike something if you never give it a chance? You can't!

If all you do is close doors all around you because you're afraid of trying something new, then all you'll do is hold yourself back, and that's a big problem. You need to be willing to try new things in order to grow.

Maybe you try a new food at a restaurant, or you decide that you'll try out for a sport you've been curious about, but are afraid of failing at. Maybe it's talking to someone new or going to a new place. The more new things you introduce to your life, the more life experience you get, and the more you grow. You should always try to push yourself out of your comfort zone. It does wonders for your confidence and teaches you to be adaptable.

Chapter 11: Facing Your Fears

We all have things we're afraid of. Maybe it's heights, spiders, or talking to new people. They make our palms feel sweaty, our hearts race, and give us that feeling of dread. Fear is a normal emotion, and it's one of the most basic ones, too. Even infants feel fear when they're in danger. It's a good thing, too! When you're afraid of something, it's your body's way of telling you that there's something wrong.

But fear can also work against us, especially when what we fear poses no threat to us. Sure, that spider on the wall might look creepy, but realistically, can it do anything to hurt you other than scare you? Probably not. At some point, you'll find yourself in a situation where it's just you and a spider, and you'll have to be able to deal with it on your own. It's something that you'll have to face at some point, whether you want to or not.

No matter what your fears are, you don't have to let them control you. When your fears control you, you find yourself in a position where you're held back. If you fear speaking in front of crowds, this can hold you back in school and at work when you're older. If you're afraid of heights, are you never going to travel to see the world because you'd have to get on an airplane?

Learning how to face your fears head-on and help yourself past them is a skill that can help you for the rest of your life. You might discover new fears later on in your life that you never knew you had, and knowing what to do about them can help.

This doesn't mean that your fears are invalid. It just means you'll have the tools to keep them from ruling your life.

Communicate Your Fears

One of the biggest tools you have to face your fears is to know how to talk about them. If you're afraid of failure, one of the most common fears people have, talk to your parents or friends about it. Tell them why you're afraid of it and why it matters so much to you. Just talking about what scares you can take away a lot of its power and help you to get past it. For example, if you were to tell your parents, "I'm really afraid I'm going to fail this test. What should I do?" they will probably comfort you and remind you that even if you fail, what matters is that you try your hardest. As long as you can do that, you've done your job, and that's what's important.

Other fears can be talked through too. Maybe you worry about your friends not liking you if you tell them the truth about something, or you're really afraid of going out in the dark to let your dog out at night. It's okay to be afraid of something. You don't have to be fearless to be a champion. You just have to be willing to face what scares you. That's what courage is.

Expose Yourself to Your Fears (In Moderation!)

Sometimes, the best way to get past a fear is to expose yourself to it. The more you expose yourself to something that scares you, the more you teach your body that there's nothing to be frightened of. For example, if you're afraid of the dark, you can sit in a dimly lit room and remind yourself that there's nothing wrong with it. You can expose yourself to higher heights and remind yourself that nothing bad is happening and that you're safe, even if you may be in close proximity to something you're afraid of.

Fears that impact your life are the ones that you need to practice facing head-on. For example, I don't like talking on the phone to strangers much. It's not something I've ever enjoyed. But, as an adult, sometimes I have to, and that's okay. I tell myself that I'll make a phone call at a set time, and I do it. It's gotten easier over time because I've exposed myself to doing it.

Sometimes, though, your fears are healthy. If you're afraid of a big dog running at you while snarling, that makes sense! It makes sense to be afraid of a stranger knocking on your door at night when you're home alone. Sometimes, that fear is a warning bell that's trying to keep you safe, and you should accept that. The more that you can accept your fears, the easier they become to deal with.

Accept Your Fears and Manage the Feeling

For fears that you just can't shake, it's okay to have them if you can manage them. For example, if you have a terrible spider phobia, you're probably never going to be fully comfortable when there's one crawling around your wall, and that's okay. You don't have to like it. You just have to not let that spider crawling around ruin your day.

Part of this is being able to accept your fears for what they are - thoughts. Fears aren't rational or logical, meaning that they don't always have to make sense. That's okay! If we didn't have fears as a species, there's a very real chance we just wouldn't exist anymore. It can stop you from deciding to cannonball off of a cliff into the ocean below or from poking at a venomous snake that looks cool when it strikes.

Because fears don't always make sense, sometimes, the best thing you can do is mindfully acknowledge that you are afraid of something without judging yourself for it. There's no need to make yourself feel bad because you're afraid of the little eight-legged creeper on the wall. Instead, focus on not letting the feeling distract you from what you're supposed to be doing.

Move on to the next task you have. Get past it while accepting that you're stressed out by whatever you're afraid of and recognizing that it's okay. Breathe. Ground yourself in the idea that you don't have to let your fear control you and move on with your day.

This can be hard at first. I like to use breathing exercises to help me get past my strong feelings when I have them. I take in a big, deep breath, then tell myself that whatever is scaring me isn't a threat and that I'm safe where I am, even if I'm afraid.

This helps me to move past my fears and get back to what I'm supposed to do, and it can help you, too.

Grounding Exercises for Fears

Grounding exercises might sound like you're going to get into trouble for something, but that couldn't be further from the truth. When you ground yourself, you're able to focus on the present moment. In one of my previous books, I introduced the concept of mindfulness. This is the ability to be present in the moment without judging what you feel or think. It's about just existing without thinking about the past or the future and appreciating the current moment for what it is, good or bad. These grounding exercises help you to be mindful in the face of fears.

Report the Situation

One technique you can use to take the fear out of a situation is to report on the situation as if you were a news reporter. This will help you take yourself away from your thoughts and feelings and replace them with the facts of the situation.

For example, if that spider on the wall is making it hard to focus, instead of thinking about all the ways that spider could bother you, you say, "I'm working on my homework right now. There's a spider on the wall, and I've been afraid of spiders in the past. Right now, I feel nervous and antsy, and I can't keep my eyes off it, but I can't get up to get help either."

When you walk yourself through the situation, you might see the obvious situation – in this case, calling for one of your parents to come help you.

Senses Exercise

One of my favorite exercises to use when my thoughts won't stop racing is a senses exercise. The main one I rely on involves engaging all five senses, one after the other. It forces me to focus on the world around me instead of what my emotions and thoughts are doing.

You'll need to count the following:

- 5 things you see

- 4 things you feel

- 3 things you hear

- 2 things you smell

- 1 thing you taste

By the end of it, I always find myself feeling much better.

Recite Your Times Tables

Fear uses the emotional part of our brains to control us. You can kick it back by activating the logical part of your brain instead. When you start forcing yourself to use the logical part, it takes back control from the emotional side. I like to recite my times tables to activate this logical part, starting with 1s and going all the way up to the 10s if I have to. In stressful situations, for example, you could start saying, "One times one is one. Two times one is two. Three times one is three." Then, work your way up to one times ten before moving on to two times two, two times three, and so on until you're feeling better and more able to face whatever you have to.

Chapter 12: Embracing the Power of Gratitude

Just as important as learning how to interact with others is learning how to reflect upon ourselves. In particular, the practice of gratitude stands out as an essential life skill that can significantly improve our quality of life. While it may not seem as immediately practical as public speaking or facing your fears, fostering a sense of gratitude has long-lasting impacts on our mindset, well-being, and relationships with others. Let's explore how.

Gratitude is all about appreciating what we have and recognizing the good in our lives. It's easy to get caught up in what we don't have, or what we want next, but remember, life isn't a race. There's plenty of time to reach our goals. Right now, let's focus on the journey, the experiences, and the people that make our lives so unique and rewarding.

Cultivate a Gratitude Attitude

Cultivating a gratitude attitude can make a world of difference in how we view our life. Instead of focusing on the negatives or what we lack, we shift our perspective to appreciate what we have. How can you do this? Start by keeping a gratitude journal. Each night, write down three things you're grateful for. They can be as simple as a delicious meal or as profound as the love of your family.

The practice of acknowledging our blessings daily can subtly shift our mindset. Over time, you'll find that you're not only noticing more positive things during your day, but also feeling happier and more fulfilled.

Share the Gratitude

Gratitude shouldn't be something we keep to ourselves. Sharing our appreciation with others can enhance our relationships and spread positivity. Did a friend help you with homework? Let them know you're grateful for their help. Did your mom make your favorite dinner? Thank her for the meal and the effort she put into it. The small act of expressing gratitude can make someone else's day brighter and make you feel good, too.

Preparing for Tough Times

Not every day will be a walk in the park. There will be times when things don't go our way, or we feel down. It's in these moments when the practice of gratitude can be most powerful. By reminding ourselves of the good in our lives, we can lift our spirits and find the strength to face our challenges. Remember, it's okay to feel upset or disappointed sometimes. But by practicing gratitude, we can help to balance those feelings with positive ones.

The Snowball Effect

Embracing gratitude might seem small at first, but over time it can create a snowball effect.

Remember building a snowman? You start by packing a little snowball in your hands. Now, imagine rolling that snowball down a snowy hill. As it rolls, it collects more and more snow, becoming larger with each turn. Before you know it, that tiny snowball has grown into a massive snow boulder! This is known as the "snowball effect" - a process that starts from an initial state of small significance, but gains momentum, becoming larger and more powerful with time.

That's exactly how gratitude works. At first, practicing gratitude might seem like that tiny snowball, hardly making any impact. But as you keep doing it, gratitude, like the snowball, starts picking up more 'snow'. You begin to notice more things to be thankful for, your brain starts focusing more on the positives, and less on the negatives. This can lead to improved mood, less stress, and better sleep. The effect grows and grows, much like our snowball rolling down the hill. So, just as you would keep rolling that snowball to make it bigger, keep practicing gratitude to increase its positive effects in your life.

Your Turn

Now it's your turn. Think about your day today. What three things can you be grateful for? Write them down and reflect on why these things made your day better. Try to do this daily, and before you know it, you'll start to notice a positive shift in your attitude and overall outlook.

Remember, gratitude isn't about ignoring the negatives in life. It's about acknowledging the positives and letting them inspire and motivate you. So, keep your heart open and your mind focused on the good. You'll be amazed at how a little bit of gratitude can go a long way.

Conclusion

Hey, kids!

You made it to the end of the book! Hopefully, as you've read, you've learned some important life skills that will prepare you to tackle anything that life will throw your way. From learning how to be self-disciplined and self-reliant to learning how to act in an emergency when you're home alone, the skills in this book all work to help you to grow as a person.

As you grow up, things will get harder. You will have more responsibilities, and that's okay! That's part of growing up. But, as you take on more responsibility, you will also gain more freedom. Responsibility comes with the opportunity to build trust and self-sufficiency. It comes with the chance for you to prove to yourself that you can do great things, too.

Remember that if you find yourself struggling with these skills, don't worry! Sometimes, you may need to seek help from other people. Yes, one of the skills we discussed was self-reliance, and that usually means being able to do things for yourself, but you don't have to do *everything* on your own. There are plenty of times when asking for help is the right answer, and the adults in your life are there to help and support you.

Each and every one of these skills gives you the chance to practice your own champion mindset, and I want you to know that you can do it. You have the power to do and be whatever you want to be in life, if you work hard and dedicate yourself to it.

So, good luck out there, kids, and don't forget to trust yourself and your ability to learn and grow!

Leave Your Feedback on Amazon

Please think about leaving some feedback via a review on Amazon. It may only take a moment, but it really does mean the world for small authors like myself :)

Even if you did not enjoy this title, please let me know the reason(s) in your review so that I may improve this title and serve you better.

From the Author

As a retired school teacher, my mission with this series is to create premium educational content for children that will help them be strong in the body, mind, and spirit via important life lessons and skills.

Without you, however, this would not be possible, so I sincerely thank you for your purchase and for supporting my life's mission.

Don't forget your free gifts!

(My way of saying thank you for your support)

Simply visit **haydenfoxmedia.com** to receive the following:

- 10 Powerful Dinner Conversations To Create Amazing Kids

- 10 Magical Affirmations To Help Kids Become Unstoppable in Life

(you can also scan this QR code)

More titles you're sure to love!

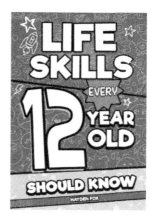

HAYDEN FOX

Printed in Great Britain
by Amazon

33637462R00076